LIFE AFTER FORECLOSURE

There is more than life after foreclosure, there is freedom.

By
RODNEY T WATSON
MARK KING

Table of Contents

Introduction

As you know the world did not come to an end. You are still alive and healthy I hope. Life continues to go on. You may not feel very smart right now after foreclosure. You lost the house and the feeling of failure and disappointment abound. For men the feeling is worse. Men are more prone to tie financial success to self-worth. Men generally take care of the family and for one reason or another we failed and lost the house.

Such is 'Life After Foreclosure.' At the time of this writing, one out of every 45 houses is in foreclosure. You can either sit and complain about it or blame other people and circumstances, or you can do something about it. It's all on how you look at it.

You can look at this as a learning experience. As a matter of fact, HOW you look at it will make all the difference in the world.

Well since we can't change the past, one thing we can do is make better choices that can affect our future in a positive way. They say that 'hindsight is 20-20.' What if you can have 20-20 vision moving forward? What if you started seeing things differently and acted differently? You must do things differently from the past or you will end up in the same position you are now. Doing things differently will produce different results.

'Watch what poor people do and don't do it. That's why they are poor.'

'Watch what rich people do and do it. That's why they are rich.'
While our focus here is not on getting rich, we want to look at how they do things so that we can have such things as positive cash flow, a higher net worth, and emergency cash reserves.

Your life can change. You can begin again. You can buy property without your credit or your own cash. You can clean up your credit the right way. You can learn how to avoid the scams and you can learn how to profit when you buy your next home.

If you can see yourself doing better, then things will work together to make it so. Knowledge will help to build your self-confidence. We will give you the knowledge. You must supply the vision. How you look at things will make all the difference in the world.

WORK SMARTER, NOT HARDER

In order not to end up on the other side of foreclosure again, it's smart to be prepared for times when you may need large sums of money. You will need to start building cash reserves. The problem is saving the money or getting the money.

Some have a hard time saving money. They make a good start. They'll get $1,000 or $2,000 in a savings account and then they see all that money just sitting there. They then want to touch it, they start to talk about it, they start to see things that the money will buy, and then the money is withdrawn and spent.

We can show you how to save the money, that's easy. What we can't do is give you your 'WHY' you should do it. Your WHY must be so strong, so large, so important, that you will stay on track come hell or high water. For example, what if someone kidnaps your loved one and tells you that all you have to do is come and get them. However, the kidnapper has your loved one 10,000 miles away in another state. How motivated will you be to get your loved one back? One hundred and ten percent!

The HOW to get there is the easy part. You can drive, fly, take a train, a boat, etc. It's the WHY that will motivate you to do whatever it takes to get them back. It's that WHY that will keep you focused on getting them back.

If you have a strong enough WHY, you can overcome any HOW.

How strong is your WHY? Is your WHY so strong that you will do whatever it takes to reach your goal? Is your WHY so strong that it alone will compel you to stay on track? Let the memory of losing your last house stay strong in your mind. Not to make you feel bad, but to motivate you to action, to motivate you not to get in that same situation again.

Find your WHY!

The Rich Man's Financial Plan

How can you save money if you make little of it? It's all how you look at your income. All the money that you bring in should not be spent haphazardly. There should be a plan for your income. Creditors should not dictate how your money is spent. You are the master of your income. You should tell your money where to go and not ask it where it went.

One way to save money is to implement the '10-10-80 Rule' for your personal finances. In the book, 'The Richest Man in Babylon' by George Clason, the first Law of Gold says that of your income;

- 10% goes to charity
- 10% goes you
- 80% is what you live on, including savings

10% - This goes to tithe or charity. This is how you 'give back.' Be grateful for what you have, no matter how little your income is.

10% - The other 10% is strictly for investments. It's only for buying assets. Assets are things that put money in your pocket. Add to this account each time you get paid. Make a habit of it. You'll see the money accumulate in this account. After a year or two you'll have more than enough money to use in case of emergency or to purchase property.

80% - This you live on. This includes savings, fun stuff, car notes, house payments, etc.

Building your cash reserve should be your first order of business. Use the second 10% to build the reserve. Keep this reserve in a different bank that is used strictly for emergencies.   It's said that you should have at least 3 months of your expenses in a reserve account. Some go as far as 1 year reserves. Whatever you do, at least keep 3 months. That amount may seem large now, however once your bills are paid off, that amount will be much less. After the reserve is built, use this 10% to build your investment account.

PAY YOURSELF FIRST - The wealthy pay themselves first. A portion of all they earn belongs to them first. This formula will also teach you to live below your means. I know it sounds hard if you are not accustomed to doing it, but if it was easy everyone would do it.
                    Find your WHY.

CASH FLOW 101

Understanding how your cash should flow is very important. Although we will not be talking about purchasing assets – you can visit my website www.RodneyTWatson.com to learn more about that – you will see that rich people have assets and poor people do not.

Assets put money IN your pocket. Liabilities take money OUT of your pocket.

On his website www.richdad.com, Robert Kiyosaki explains the cash flow pattern of 3 types of people; the poor, the middle class, and the rich. We will briefly look at each one. Which one are you in? Which one would you like to be in?

JOB

Income

Expenses

Assets | Liabilities

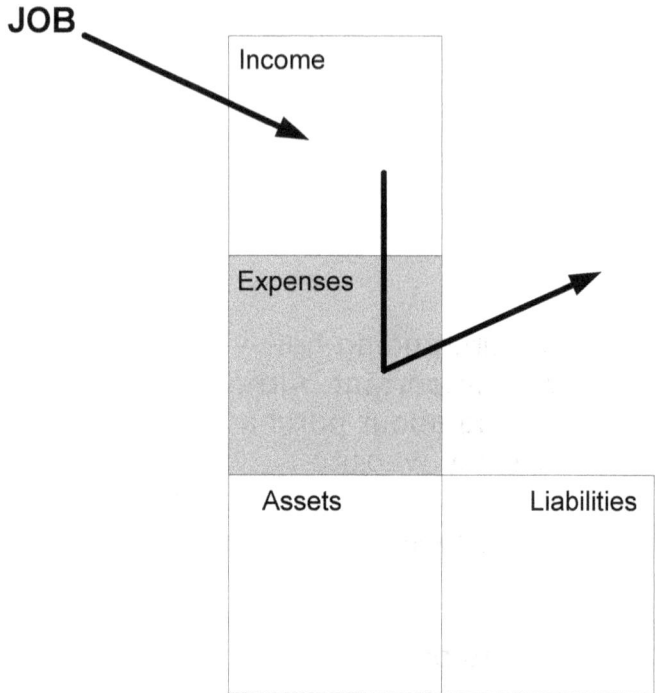

Cash Flow of the Poor.

Robert Kiyosaki, RichDad.com

This person has a job, car, small apartment. Most of the money goes to pay expenses like rent, food, clothes, car and most of all taxes. Many young people begin this way.

Most of their money is taken by Uncle Sam to pay taxes. They get very little tax breaks.

JOB

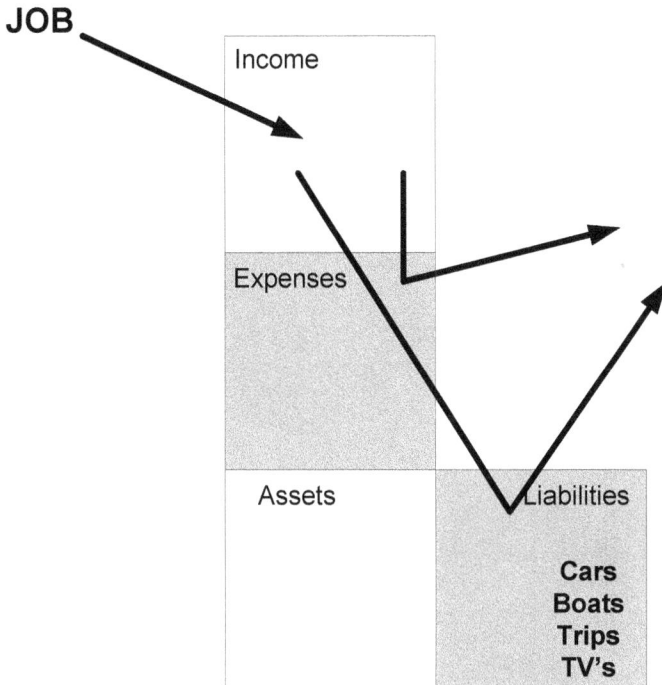

Income

Expenses

Assets

Liabilities

Cars
Boats
Trips
TV's

Cash Flow of the Middle Class.

Robert Kiyosaki, RichDad.com

The middle class usually have a good paying job. So they make a little more money. In fact, the more money they earn the more stuff they can buy and the more stuff they do buy. A bigger raise means a bigger car, a bigger boat, a bigger house, and better trips. Most are living paycheck to paycheck.

If that job goes away, so will all that stuff. They have the look of wealth, but have the finances of the poor. These are the guys with the boats, recreational vehicles, and nice cars. They are using their earned income to purchase depreciating liabilities.

Notice that the arrows are pointing away from the Income column. All the money coming in is going out. Many take refuge in the fact that they are saving money by putting it in a mutual fund. Often that is their only source of savings. By the way, the rich don't invest in mutual funds.

This class also pays high taxes and gets very few tax breaks.

JOB

Income

Expenses

Assets   Liabilities

Rentals   **Cars**
Business   **Boats**
                          Trips
                          TV's

Cash Flow of the Rich.

Robert Kiyosaki, RichDad.com

The rich or those on that path, defer immediate self gratification. They use their earned income to buy assets. They then use the profits from the assets to buy more assets. This way their money is now making more money. Hence the rich get richer.

The rich also use their asset money to purchase liabilities or fun stuff. So now when they buy that car, it does not affect their monthly budget. At some point many will stop working and let their assets make money and pay for their liabilities or fun stuff. The income from the rentals is called Passive Income.

They pay lower taxes and get hundreds of tax breaks.

Which type would you like to be?

Then Find Your WHY!

GOOD DEBT - *BAD DEBT*

Did you notice the cash flow of the rich? They owned rental properties. This means that they took out a loan on those houses. They now owe the bank hundreds of thousands of dollars which they pay back in monthly installments. They are heavily in debt. Is this good debt or bad debt?

If they have to pay it back out of their own pocket, it's bad debt. If they have tenants that are paying rent, it's good debt. Very good debt is when someone pays your debt and gives you hundreds of dollars on top of that. That's called positive cash flow.

Stay away from bad debt. Bad debt is credit cards that you have to pay back. Credit cards are good if someone else is paying the bill. Bad debt is anything that charges you more for goods than the value of the goods.

The rich have bills, but their assets are paying the bills. The rich have to send their kids to college, so they use their assets to pay for it. They use their cash flowing assets to help pay for many things that normal people pay straight out their pocket for.

There are certain assets that when purchased makes you a business owner. As a business owner, you will get tax breaks that you would normally not receive. Low taxes are a good thing since your largest expense in life will be taxes. You will pay more in taxes over your life time than anything else in life.

"Money may not bring happiness, but neither does poverty."

LIFE IS LIKE MONOLOPY

Remember playing the board game Monopoly? It taught us how to get rich by building wealth through buying real estate. Monopoly teaches that there are 3 types of income:

1. Earned Income – pass 'Go' collect $200.
2. Portfolio Income – receive dividends from stocks.
3. Passive Income – income from rental properties and businesses.

1. EARNED INCOME: This comes from your job. We show up, do some work, and get paid. Often we are happy just to make it through the week. Many continue in this cycle all their lives. They keep passing 'Go' collecting paycheck after paycheck, never achieving the financial success they desire.

2. PORTFOLIO INCOME: These are your 401k plans, IRAs, mutual funds, etc. Portfolio income is good. However, the problem is that you can't touch your money until some 20 to 30 years out. Even then, you are hoping the interest rates are low once you cash out. Do you really want to wait that long for your hard earned money? Do you really want to live on a fixed income? That's like passing 'Go' all over again...the same $200 each payday. Your income should grow as your age grows. The older you get, the richer you should get.

3. PASSIVE INCOME: This represents income from property or owning a business. How did you achieve financial success in Monopoly? By buying property and collecting rent. You bought 4 houses and then turned them into a hotel. Then the big money came in. You didn't really need to pass 'Go' anymore. You were financially independent. Didn't it feel good to have such a great cash flow? Well, it works this way in real life too.

!!!NEWS FLASH!!!

"IN THE GAME OF LIFE EVERYONE PLAYS MONOPOLY"
You're either Passing GO or you're buying property/business.

Monopoly Mirrors Real Life.
The US Department of Health, Education, and Welfare tracked people from age 20 to 65. Their findings were as follows:

Out of every 100 people studied, by age 65:

- 1% was wealthy

- 4% were well-off

- 5% were still working because they had to

- 54% were living on family or government support

- 36% were dead

Where will you be at age 65? Most important, who are the 1% wealthy and how did they do it?

Here's a breakdown on that 1%:

- 74% Business Owner/Real Estate Investor

- 10% Doctor/Attorney

- 10% CEO/President

- 5% Salesperson

- 1% Lottery/Inheritance

As you can see, if you don't have real estate as a part of your portfolio, you may never be a part of that 1%. **Playing Monopoly without buying property is crazy**. How could you ever expect to win the game? Well it's the same in real life. Just passing 'GO' will never give you the wealth needed to be in that 1%.

97% of all millionaires received their money through real estate!

These millionaires continued playing Monopoly while the vast majority settled for the easy route of passing 'Go.' Well, it's time to take up the game again. It's time to stop taking the easy route that leads to financial dependence. It's time to do some work and take some risks. It's time to take the road towards financial freedom.

"Monopoly gives people the clearest 'view' of how life should be lived."

In Monopoly you bought property and held on to it. On that piece of land you built a house. Then you added another house and so on. Soon the money from your houses helped you to buy even more houses. Your assets were buying assets. You became very wealthy. It happens the same way in real life.

Remember that **'Go to Jail'** square in Monopoly? As a kid I would amass much property. Then I would try my best to land in jail. This way I wouldn't have to pay rent to the other players and I could still collect rent. In real life it represents getting laid off, getting sick, being unable to work, downsized, or whatever causes you to stop working. In the real world any of these scenarios may happen to you, God forbid. Buying and holding property can be the means to sustain you during these down times. In the game, you can still collect rent while in jail; in real life you can still collect rent while you are out of a job.

All your houses are potential income producing assets. This income becomes a part of your income cash flow. This is called 'multiple streams of income.' Christians call this 'showers of blessings.'

By now real estate may have left a nasty taste in your mouth and you want nothing to do with it. Yes, there are risks. However, the rich take a calculated risk. They get educated on the subject and go for it. You will notice that during down times the rich get richer. When everyone is selling, they are buying. When everyone is buying, they are selling. You can do the same thing. All you need is some education. We will discuss this later in the book.

We hope that you are starting to look at things differently now. You must see the other side of money to appreciate its flow. Money will either flow through you to others thus making them rich and leaving you poor or money will flow through you making you rich and help to enrich the lives of others. Learn to cooperate with money. Let it work for you. Let it help others. Most of all let it build a firm financial foundation for you and your family. In this way you will stand firm during the next down turn. Yes, there will always be down turns. However, since you know it's coming, you can be prepared for it.

Do things different from what you did in the past. Develop a passion to live better, work better, save better. **Most of all find your WHY!**

Develop a plan for your life, a written plan. An unwritten plan is impossible to follow.

Your goals or vision allows you to visit your future so that you are motivated to leave your present.

FIND YOUR WHY!!!

How to Buy Your Next House

You have heard the adage, *'there is more than one way to skin a cat.'* (No offense to cats) Well, when buying houses the same is true. There is more than one way to buy a house. There are 3 common ways you can get into your next house:

1. Lease Option to Buy
2. Owner Financing
3. Equity Sharing

You can lease a house and option to purchase it later. The owner can carry the note and you can purchase the home over time without using a bank. Much of this is called creative financing.

It may be a while before many lenders will be willing to take a chance and lend you money. Congress may pass some laws to help the thousands going into foreclosure each year. Until that happens, you must learn how to obtain property without good credit and with little money. You need to learn about lease options.

WHAT IS AN OPTION? An option is an agreement to by a property at a point in time, for a certain price, with defined terms. An option is the right to buy, not an obligation to buy.

1. Lease-Option to Buy
With Lease/Purchase you are still a Tenant who has the Option, or right to buy a house

within a specific period of time, typically during your Lease term.

You have the benefits of possession and a guaranteed pre-agreed upon price of the home you will eventually own. But you don't have financial benefits, such as mortgage loan interest deduction, property tax deduction, mortgage balance pay down, etc.

Lease-purchase is common. You sign a lease agreement with the current owner that has terms that say a portion of your lease payment will be credited toward the down payment when you buy the house at a stated price at a stated date in the future. See sample contract in Appendix.

Make sure the following information is in the lease option contract:

Identification of the property – Get a copy of the Deed and write down the legal description of the property. You also need to see this to make sure that the person you are talking to is really the owner.

Expiration date - The contract should have an ending date. At that time you must either buy the house, leave the house, or renew the option.

Purchase price – Make sure the agreed upon price is written. Only what is on paper counts.

$$$ Consideration – In most cases, you will need to pay a non-refundable fee to begin the option. The fee amount may be different according to the deal. You may be asked to pay $1,000 to $5,000 for the option.

Think of this as Earnest Money. The owner just wants to make sure you are serious about keeping your end of the contract. Get everything in writing. Make no verbal contract. This will protect both of you from misunderstandings. **Make sure that you are able to collect your original option money if the property goes into foreclosure in the event the owner stops making payments.** This doesn't happen often; still you want to cover all bases.

Note: Lease payments for a personal residence are not tax-deductible and there is no pay down on loan principal, it is just money going to someone else for the use of the space.

BEWARE OF REAL ESTATE SCAMS - The most common scam happens either during or after the foreclosure. A person breaks into a vacant house, changes the locks and then rents the property out. When a property is advertised at below market rent, the phone number goes to a voice mail and the "landlord" wants to meet at a restaurant or other public place, it's quite likely a scam.

Ask to meet at the house and ask to see the Deed. Go to your local County Records Office to verify the owners.

Another variation on this same theme is a person giving an owner in foreclosure a cash amount for the equity in the home. The small cash payment gains control of the property which is then rented out with no payments made to the lender. The "landlord" pockets any rents received while delaying the foreclosure as long as possible.

Do your own due diligence.

2. Owner Financing

Owner financing (also called seller financing or owner carry-back) is when the seller of a property allows the buyer to pay all or some of the purchase price over time. You may have seen signs saying '100% Owner Financing,' 'No Money Down,' 'Seller Financing,' 'No Banks' and so forth.

Typically, the transaction is set up as a private mortgage which means that the seller holds a lien on the property – just like a bank. Remember, you are buying the property over time.

Owner financing is an excellent way for a buyer and seller to work together. Here is a simplified example that illustrates how it could work. Let's say I have a house to sell and you want to buy it:

Asking price of house: $150,000
Current first mortgage: $100,000
Money you have saved: $ 20,000

The difference is $30,000. If you are able to assume the first mortgage, I can "lend" the remaining $30,000 to you and register it as a second mortgage on the property. Then you would make 2 regular mortgage payments - to the bank on the first mortgage and to me on the second.

Some Advantages of Owner Financing to the Seller

- Getting a top price by taking terms rather than all cash
- Deferring taxes now on any gain by using an installment sale
- Receiving a higher interest rate than if you put the proceeds from a cash sale in the bank, a CD, or Money Market account
- Monthly income secured by property you understand and whose value you know

You can get into one of these if you know you want to buy that house. This is very similar to Lease Option. The difference is that the owner will act as the bank, thus giving you an interest rate, checking your credit, offering lower closing costs. You are basically bypassing the bank and using the owners existing financing. You won't be on the loan, you won't own the house, yet you will be making the owners mortgage payments.

Owners who can't sell their property often will use this to help pay the mortgage. It's better for them to have someone else paying some of the mortgage and they pay the rest, than to have to pay the full amount themselves.

The Owner may charge you a higher interest rate so there may be positive cash flow for the owner. The extra money they may use for repairs and so forth.

Again make sure you get everything in writing. You should have someone look at the contract for you. Owner financing can be tricky if you don't know what you are doing. Make sure you review the contract carefully.

Since you are buying the property over time, the length of the contract can be more than 10 years. Lease option contracts typically don't go out more than 2 years. You must decide how quickly you can get back on your feet. If you need a few years, do a lease option. If you need any more than that, try owner financing.

During the lease term, work on your financial portfolio, save your cash reserves and establish your credit.

3. How to Purchase Property Through Equity Sharing

What is Equity Sharing? - 'When 2 or more persons pool their money together to purchase property, for the purpose dividing the equity money between them after the property has accumulated enough equity to be sold or refinanced.'

'Credit is Better Than Cash'

Some people have cash but no credit. Others have credit, but no cash. Put these two together and you have: An Investor(s) (cash partner) & The Qualifier (credit partner).

When you want to buy an investment property or a property for yourself, and don't have the cash, but your credit is good, you need one or more cash investors. The investor(s) will put up all the cash required. However, your good credit will secure the property.

Here's how it works: For example: say you found a house that costs 125k. The down payment plus closing costs are 10k. The investor(s) will have to come up with the entire 10k. You and the investor are bound together by an Equity Share agreement. According to this agreement, your group will sit on the property and wait for it to appreciate in value. Once the house appreciates at a level acceptable to the group, it can be sold or equity can be taken out.

Say the house now has 100k equity in it. If you did a cash-out-refi or a HELOC, the investor would first get their 10k back, and then the rest of the money would be split equally. Both the qualifier and the investor would get 45k each. Depending on where you buy this can happen within 5 years.

You can also be an investor along with the other investors. If you have $2,000, and four other investors have $2,000, you'll have 10,000 which is more than enough for the down payment and closing cost on a house up to $125,000 in most states. However, one person in the group will have to be the qualifier.

Most people start out this way. They will purchase a property by equity sharing with a group. They wait a few years for the property to appreciate, and then do a cash-out-refi on the property. The group then divides the money equally. Each member of the group will receive their initial investment - $2,000 – then their share of the equity.

That $2,000 investment could easily turn into $20,000 in less than 5 years. Of course that depends on how well you selected the property. With that tax-free money you can then begin to build your own real estate empire and pay off a few bills too.

Finding an Equity Share Group.

Real Estate Clubs are your safe and best bets when trying to locate investors. The newspaper is full of investors willing to equity share. However, they are often into the 'big bucks' and may not bother with such small investments.

Your family members can equity share with you. Make it a family affair.

Your uncle, brother, in-laws, mom, and dad, can be in your group. If they have the money, why not? Then you can keep the property in the family. Most of all, you will help build the wealth of your family members. This way they won't have to live off of your wealth later.

CAUTION- Sometimes it's better to keep family and business matters separate. Ill feelings can occur over bad deals or if one family member doesn't keep up their end of the bargain. The last thing you want is to tear your family apart over money and houses. So tread very carefully before approaching your family to equity share.

YOUR EQUITY SHARE GROUP

Your group should consist of 5 to 6 persons. Couples are counted as one person. Each person needs have $3,000 to invest. At least one person in the group should be able to qualify for the loan.

Your goals and objectives are to:
- Pick a qualifier for the group
- Pick a treasurer
- Establish and maintain a bank account
- Research and find properties
- Purchase 1 property

1. Select 1 or 2 persons to qualify for the loan. *See requirements for qualifier below.*
2. Select a person to be treasurer. This person will open an account and pay the mortgage each month. This account is not the one which the initial monies go into.
3. $3,000 from each investor goes into the qualifier's account to show the lender. Excess money will go to the treasurer for the main account.
4. Establish the max amount to bid for property, i.e.: 100k to 125k

Once you agree on a property, call the agent for the sales contract. The $3,000 from each person should be in the qualifiers account.

THE QUALIFIER

In order to qualify for property you must *generally* have the following:

Good Monthly Income – At least 2 years solid work history

Assets to Cover Loan – Bank accounts, 401k plans, IRA's, $13,000 in your account for 2 months, 1 month in most cases.

Reserve – 2 to 6 months of money to cover possible loss, about 6k.

Tips: You don't have to have perfect credit, but you must have something to work with. If you can't do it alone, take on a partner. You can put 2 people on the loan. This means you'll have 2 qualifiers. The two of you will be on the Deed as well. Choose 2 people with good work histories, and a decent credit score.

To check your credit score go to "myfico.com."   Click on 'The Short View.' There you can get your credit pulled for $15. The best part is that it won't affect your credit. It's a good way to see your scores without the ding to your credit.

THE EQUITY SHARE AGREEMENT CONTRACT

Your group will have to fill out an equity share agreement contract for each property the group purchases. This agreement will detail the following:

- Each person's contact info
- The amount of each person's contribution
- Each person's equity share amount
- Terms of buy-out
- Terms of early out due to death, divorce, and hardship
- Other terms and conditions

Make sure you get the agreement notarized. You can use this agreement to show your tax preparer so he/she can make the proper tax deductions, if applicable.

You can email me for a free electronic copy of a sample contract. ***Under the advice of an attorney, you can use the form for your own use.***

My email address is: orodneyo@hotmail.com

Credit Reports:
What You Need to Know

It is estimated that 80% of all credit reports have bad, false, or misleading information contained within them. However, a significant number of Americans have never seen a copy of their credit report. Many consumers spend countless hours wondering why they were turned down for credit, not knowing that there were mistakes on their credit report. It is not uncommon for someone else's negative marks to be posted to our credit file simply because they have a similar name or social security number.

Get a current copy of your credit report. Don't assume that every bad credit experience you've ever had will appear on your credit report. There are many companies that don't report their losses to credit bureaus.

To get copies of your credit report, contact the three major credit bureaus: Experian Inc. (formally TRW), Trans Union Corp., and Equifax Inc., to see which agency has a file on you. Don't just write to one. Write to all three. These agencies are competing businesses and they do not share information with each other. So it is in your best interest to find out what each one of them knows about you.

You might also want to contact your local credit bureaus, because there may be several different copies of your credit report floating around. Experian Inc., Trans Union Corp., and Equifax Inc., are the three largest, so start with them. The address of each credit bureau is listed below:

Experian Inc.	Trans Union	Equifax Inc.
PO Box 2104	Corp.	PO Box 4081
Allen, TX	PO Box 2000	Atlanta, GA
75013	Chester, PA	30309
1.800.682.76	19022	1.800.685.11
54	1.800.916.88	11
	00	

Note: Companies will periodically change their address or phone number. If you find any of the above information to be incorrect, contact your local better business bureau for the correct information.

Write to each credit bureau and request that they send you a copy of your credit report. (See Appendix Letter 1). Currently all three credit bureaus charge $8 for a copy of your report. If you have been denied credit within the past 30 days you are entitled to receive a free copy of your credit report from the credit bureau that issued your information under the protection of the Fair Credit Report Act. Explain this in your letter. (See Appendix Letter 2).

How to Control Creditors

Make sure you communicate with all your creditors. Try to call them before you miss a payment and let them know you need help. With credit card companies, try to negotiate a reduced payment plan with them for a few months. But don't make arrangements you will not be able to keep.

Be honest and upfront. Most creditors are willing to help you if you come to them before things get bad.

If you can't pay an unsecured creditor, like a credit card company, don't worry about it. They can't take you to jail for not paying them. Usually, what happens is that they send your account to a collection agency after your account has been delinquent for more than 120 days.

Most collection agencies will call and harass you morning and night until they get their money. They will tell you how they will ruin your credit and attack your wages. Don't worry, you can fix any bad credit you get and they can't attack your wages without taking you to court and winning a judgment.

They may even call you at work. To stop them from calling you at home or work all you have to do is send them a certified letter stating that you want them to stop calling you at work and at home; remind them of your right to sue for a violation of your rights granted to you by the Fair Credit Reporting Act.

A Direct Plea to the Creditor

If you have dug yourself into a financial hole that you can't get out of, then a direct plea to the creditor may be a good choice for you. Believe it or not, this approach catches creditors off guard. Most creditors are even wiling to work out a settlement with you because of your honesty about your situation. Usually, they will accept a small percentage of your balance as payment-in-full on your account. After all, they are in business to make money, not lose it. So, even a small amount of money to a creditor is better than no money at all.

The following is a sample letter after which you may pattern your own.

'Dear Sir/Madam,

I recently received your letter notifying me that my account, #123-ABC with you is currently past due. I have made every attempt to meet this payment. Unfortunately, due to unforeseen circumstances in my family, I am unable to make good on my current payments at the rate previously agreed to at this time.

I am certain however, that my financial situation will improve in the near future and at that time, I will be able to resume payments to you at the agreed schedule.

In the interim, I am enclosing a token payment of $XX.XX to show my good intentions.

Sincerely,

Joe Q. Customer'

Please note that a letter has a greater impact than a phone call. However, the one drawback to sending a letter is that it can become legally binding so be careful regarding any promises made.

If you find yourself constantly bombarded with harassing phone calls from creditors or collection agencies, then threatening to sue might be a good way to stall them for a considerable amount of time. First, you need to know when it's a good time to "cry wolf."

It is the job of the Federal Trade Commission (FTC) to oversee most credit buying practices. The FTC is also responsible for insuring that consumers are not harassed by creditors or collection agencies. Unfortunately, harassment has become the preferred method most creditors use to collect past due payments. Federal, State and local laws prohibit such tactics.

The laws that govern harassment are very clear about what creditors and collection agencies can and cannot do. The law says that a creditor is forbidden to communicate or even threaten to communicate with a debtor's employer, until a final judgment has been obtained in court. A collection agency may not send dunning letters to a debtor that threatens to damage the debtor's credit rating, threatens certain legal actions, or threatens certain criminal action. Any threat of criminal action is illegal. A collection agency may not use a name that misleads someone to think that they are some government agency. In addition, they may not falsely represent themselves as a lawyer, law enforcement agency, or private detective. Collection agencies are also prohibited from calling on, or otherwise contacting a third party such as a neighbor or employer to discuss your debt.

The Federal Communication Commission (FCC) has ruled that it is illegal for a creditor or collection agency to use the telephone to abuse, harass, or otherwise frighten a debtor; they may not call the debtor's home and discuss his/her debt with an unauthorized family member. If you feel that a creditor violated your rights by use of the telephone, notify the FCC and your local telephone company.

> Federal Communication
> Commission (FCC)
> 1919 M. Street NW
> Washington, DC 20554

All of the above mentioned tactics are covered by the Fair Credit Reporting Act, amended September 30, 1996. If you would like to receive a copy, please write to the Public Reference Branch, Federal trade Commission, Washington, DC 20580. Or you can write to your local Federal Trade Commission regional office. Listed below are the regional offices of the Federal Trade Commission:

> 730 Peachtree St., Atlanta, GA
> 30308
> John F. Kennedy Federal Building,
> Boston, MA 02203

55 E. Monroe St., Suite 1860,
Chicago, IL 60604-1073
1240 E. Ninth St., Cleveland, OH
44199
500 S. Ervay St., Dallas, TX 75201
911 Walnut St., Kansas City, MO
64203
11000 Wilshire Blvd., Suite 13209,
Los Angeles, CA 90024
25 Federal Plaza, New York, NY
10007
901 Market Street, Suite 570, San
Francisco, CA 94103
1511 Third Ave., Seattle, WS
98101
2120 L Street, NW Washington,
DC 20037

If you feel that a creditor has violated your rights, then send them a letter similar to the one below. In your letter, explain that your rights were violated and that you intend to sue. It is advisable that you also send letters to any of the above mentioned agencies if it is appropriate. See sample letter below.

The following is a sample letter after which you may pattern your own.

Dear Sir/Madame:

"On November 5, 2007, I received a letter from you stating your intentions of profaning my credit if I did not make a payment of $XX.XX that you claim is now past due. Furthermore, on November 30, 2007, a representative of your company acting on your behalf, telephoned my home and discussed an alleged debt with an unauthorized member of my family.

Your practice was defamation to my character and an invasion of my privacy. I will not permit my family or myself to be subjected to your illegal tactics. Continued harassment by you will result in my immediate filing of a law suit against your company for damages.

Sincerely,

Joe Q. Customer"

A letter such as the one above can be very effective in stalling a creditor or even getting them to write off your debt completely. It will give a creditor the impression that you know your rights. Most creditors, when confronted with a knowledgeable consumer, are reluctant to pursue any further action against that individual for fear of a law suit.

No creditor wants to be tied up in a law suit with a knowledgeable consumer. Especially if they know that it will cost them more to take the case to trial. If there is a collection agency involved, you can be confident that most creditors will write the case off as "uncollectible," because they know that even if they won in court, the collection agency will get half (50%) of their judgment. So unless the amount involved is extremely large (greater than $10,000), most creditors won't even bother with further collection attempts and forget and about you... maybe.

You may be asking yourself, "If they write off my account as 'uncollectible,' can't they report the incident to a credit reporting bureau and ruin my credit?" The answer is NO! It was their decision to drop the claim against you. All you did was challenge the legality of their certain business practices. They felt that it was in their best interest to write off our case, so they lose any claims that they had against you.

Bargaining Your Way Out of Debt

If done properly, bargaining can wipe out all your debt at one time, for a fraction of the total amount you owe. You might want to use this approach even if you can make your monthly payments, but don't want to anymore. This approach falls short of threatening bankruptcy.

First - make a list of all your unsecured creditors and how much you owe them. This means that your home mortgage and car payment won't be included.

Second - decide how much you are willing to settle your entire debt for.

Third - go out and get as much money as you can from friends and relatives. Let's assume that you have five creditors, your total debt is $10,000, and you were able to raise $2,000. With a few math calculations, you realize that you can repay each creditor 20% of what you owe. *(Note: the more money you raise, the greater the likelihood of your creditors accepting your settlement.)*

If you can get one of your friends or someone else to work with you on this plan it will have a better effect on your creditors. If you can get a lawyer to help you, that would be even better. Using a third party gives the impression that for some unknown reason, you are unable to manage your own affairs. This will cause your creditors to think that maybe they will be unable to collect from you and that they would be better off getting whatever they can.

Type a separate letter to each individual creditor. If you're using an attorney, they will know how to draft the contents of such a letter. Below is a sample letter that you may refer to when drafting your own.

The following is a sample letter after which you may pattern your own.

"Dear Sir/Madam:

I have been retained by [or represent] Mr./Mrs. Joe Q. Customer [and/or, his/her family] for the purpose of settling as many of his/her outstanding debts as possible before filing a petition of bankruptcy.

Mr./Mrs. Customer's total debts at present total $10,000 with assets of negligible value.

In an effort to honorably settle with his/her creditors, Mr./Mrs. Customer has managed to raise $2,000 for this purpose. The money will be distributed on an equal percentage basis among the five creditors who accept this offer. Your percentage may be as little as 20%

dependent upon the number of creditors who find this offer acceptable.

The funds in the settlement of debts due will be mailed on _____. *(Write in the date 10 days from the time you mail this letter to the creditor.)* Your response must be received prior to this date.

To accept this offer, please sign the enclosed copy of this letter and return it to me using the enclosed self-addressed stamped envelope.

Pursuant to the provisions stated above, we hereby agree to accept a minimum of $XX.XX or a greater amount pursuant to the number of creditors accepting this offer as full payment and settlement on account number 123-ABC.

Name of creditor

_____
Authorized Signature

_____
Date _____ "

A letter drafted along the lines of the one above can be very effective. None of the creditors want to be the one left out of the deal. Therefore, each one will take the position of "let some other creditor be the loser." They know that there's a chance that they will only receive 20% of their money.

However, by the same token, there's always the chance that they can receive much more, and creditor's, by nature, love to gamble; they will jump at your offer because they know that it is better to get some money than to get no money at all.

The Truth about Credit Repair Agencies

If you pick up a newspaper in any big city across America, there is a good chance that you will see an ad for a Credit Repair Agency. Whether they are called Credit Counseling Companies, Credit Restoration Firms, Credit Clinics, or Credit Repair Agencies, they all promise the same thing – the complete restoration of your credit report.

Most consumers don't have a clue as to how these companies fix credit. Usually, an individual with a poor credit rating will contact a credit repair agency in the hopes that they can remove all of the negative marks off your credit report. The credit repair agency assumes the role of middleman between you, your creditors, and the Credit Bureau.

The credit repair agency will meet with you to discuss your situation, and then begin a systematic letter-writing campaign to clear up your credit report. This letter writing process will continue until most or all of your negative items have been removed from your credit report. At this point, you will be counseled on how to get positive items posted to your credit.

In most cases the agency will be successful in repairing most of your credit. However, their services are not cheap. Typically, they charge $500 to $1,500 and there is nothing magical about what they do. It's not a matter of luck or who you know, either. So what is it then? How do these agencies manage to fix your credit report?

They use the same information and techniques outlined below. Within these pages, you will find everything you need to know about repairing you own credit. It is complete with step-by-step instructions to help guide you from start to finish.

The 9 Steps to Credit Repair

Repairing your credit takes nine steps, each of which will be discussed in greater detail in the next few pages.

1. Obtain a copy of your credit report from the three major credit bureaus (Experian, Trans Union Corp., and Equifax).

2. Highlight all negative items.

3. Challenge each of the negative items.

4. Request an updated credit report; check to ensure that some of the negative items were removed.

5. Repeat steps 2-4 once every two months until no additional items are removed.

6. Prepare a consumer statement disputing each of the remaining negative items, and request that the Credit Bureau include the statement in your credit file.

7. Request that each Credit Bureau furnish you with the names and addresses of each creditor still reporting a negative entry for your account.

8. Contact each of these creditors and attempt to negotiate a settlement.

9. Request that updated copies of your credit report be sent to anybody who

received your credit report in the past six months.

These steps are all based on the rights granted to consumers through the Fair Credit Reporting Act (FRCA). As you implement the steps outlined above do note that the FCRA will not protect any request, challenge, or consumer statement that can be proven to be frivolous in nature.

It is highly unlikely that this charge will be made by a creditor or credit bureau, as they know that your defense can be that you were simply acting according to your understanding of your rights as granted by the FCRA.

Step One: Get a Copy of Your Credit Report

Before you can start to fix your credit report, you must first figure out what it contains. If you still have your credit reports that I suggested you get at the beginning of this book, go to step 2. If you don't have a copy of your report, then do the following:

Contact the three major credit bureaus, Experian Inc., Trans Union Corp., and Equifax Inc., to see which agency has a file on you. You might also want to contact other local credit bureaus, because there may be several different versions of your credit report floating around. It is a good idea to start with the three major credit bureaus and deal with others later.

Experian Inc.	Trans Union	Equifax Inc.
PO Box 2104	Corp.	PO Box 4081
Allen, TX	PO Box 2000	Atlanta, GA
75013	Chester, PA	30309
1.800.682.76	19022	1.800.685.11
54	1.800.916.88	11
	00	

Write to each credit bureau and request that they send you a copy of your credit report (See Appendix Letter 1). Currently all three credit bureaus charge $8.00 for a copy of our report. However, if you have been denied credit within the past 30 days you are entitled to receive a free copy of your credit report from the credit bureau that issued your information.

In your letter to the credit bureau, explain that under the protection of the Fair Credit Report Act you are entitled to a free copy of your credit report, if you have been denied credit in the past 30 days (See Appendix Letter 2).

If you went to a credit repair agency, they will ask you to apply for credit in hopes that you will be rejected. As such, they will be able to send for your credit report without having to pay the fee required for each report.

Although you may save $8.00, in your effort to repair your credit, you don't need any unnecessary credit denials added to your credit report at this time. This is the exact kind of information that you are trying to erase from your file. However, if you don't have the $24.00 necessary to buy all three copies of your credit reports, this is an option.

There are other ways of learning about your credit report. Instead of the letter request, you can call the Credit Bureau and make an appointment to review your credit file in person. It is advisable that you wait for the Credit Bureau to tell you everything they know about your credit history before you volunteer any potentially damaging information to other parties.

Step Two: Note All Negative Items on the Report

Each Credit Bureau has their own way of organizing their credit reports. Make sure that you read and understand all the information they send on how to read their report. It is up to you to determine which entries are damaging.

Such items may include a different social security number, incorrect name or spelling of your name, wrong addresses, and excessive number of inquiries, charge offs, late payments, judgments, or anything else that will keep you from being granted new credit.

Perhaps your record was confused with another customer who has a similar name or social security number. Maybe the negative information is outdated, beyond the seven year legal reporting limit imposed by the FCRA.

Step Three: Challenge Each of the Negative Items

Send letters to each Credit Bureau, challenging each of the negative items on your report, even though they may be true (See Appendix Letter 3).The Fair Credit Reporting Act (FRCA) states that any credit item that is challenged by a consumer must be proven by the creditor in order to be considered verified.

If this re-verification is not completed in a timely manner (approximately 30 days) or if the challenge goes unanswered, the affected negative credit items must be completely deleted from your file, never to reappear.

Note: *Do not challenge more than four items at a time. Challenging more than four may cause the Credit Bureau to deem your challenge frivolous and deny your challenge.*

Your challenges can be based on the argument that:

- You never made late payments to that account

- The account is not yours

- You don't remember the facts as stated on your credit report

- You don't remember applying for the credit card

There may be other arguments applicable to your particular situation. The challenging process works very well because there are many factors working to your benefit:

- Certain negative items cannot be proven because they were legitimately in error and should have never been reported in the first place

- Credit denials are often thrown out by creditors soon after they are received. As such, these items are generally not reconfirmed. Also, if the item is over two years old, there is a good chance that these records are not retained by the creditor.

- If you have already paid off the account, the creditor will probably not want to be bothered and will not respond to the challenge.

- A creditor might not respond within the time constraints set by the credit bureau in accordance with the FCRA's guidelines, generally about 30 days.

There is also the element of human error that can come into play (i.e. they may lose the challenge report, can't find the proof, things get lost in the mail, etc.) and result in a non-response by the creditor. The end result: the items are removed from your report. So, the odds are in your favor.

Step Four: Receive an Updated Credit Report

Within one month of challenging any negative items, you should receive an updated copy of your credit report (hopefully without some of the old negative items). If you have not received your new report within 6 weeks, call the credit bureau and remind them that you are waiting for the new copy of your credit report.

Step Five: Repeat this Procedure Once Every Two Months

Keep repeating steps 2 through 4 every two months until no additional items are removed as a result of your challenges. If the remaining creditors are determined to reconfirm their claims and continue to do so over and over again, it is time to move on to the next step.

Step Six: Prepare a Consumer Statement

Prepare a 100-word statement of dispute for each of the remaining negative items, and have the Credit Bureau include these statements in your credit file. These statements will show that the situation is still in dispute, and that there is another side to the story. You won't be declared unworthy of credit based on these claims, because they are still pending (See Appendix Letter 4).

Step Seven: Request the Names and Addresses of Each Creditor

Explain to the Credit Bureau that there are still many mistakes on your credit report and that you would like to contact the creditors in question directly. Request that the Bureau send you the names, addresses, and phone numbers of each creditor still reporting a negative entry for your account (See Appendix Letter 5).

Step Eight: Contact Each Creditor and Negotiate a Settlement

Negotiations between each creditor may differ depending on the circumstances. Creditors of unsecured loans are motivated to settle because after a certain amount of time these accounts are written off as a total loss; any payments would be considered to be "found" money, so you will probably have a very willing negotiating partner (See Appendix Letter 6).

Step Nine: Ask That They Send Out Your Updated Credit Report

When your credit report is as clean as it's going to get, contact each Credit Bureau one more time. Request that updated copies of your credit report, be sent to all the creditors who received a copy of your credit report within the past six months (See Appendix Letter 7).

How to Build a Good Credit Rating

While you are removing all or most of the negative items from your credit report, you will need to add some positive marks to it. Believe it or not, it is fairly simple to add positive marks to your credit report and it doesn't require that you keep a close track of what kind of information is posted to your credit report.

Often our good behavior is not reflected on our credit report, yet this is exactly the type of behavior that we want the creditors to see because it is crucial to building a good credit reputation.

A good rating is implied by the absence of negative information. To be considered a good credit risk, you need to concentrate on positive information and bring it to the attention of creditors.

There is a good chance that our credit report does not contain information about all of the accounts that you have with creditors. Although most major department stores and credit card accounts will be included in your report, not all creditors supply information to credit bureaus.

There are some gasoline card companies, credit unions, and local retailers that do not report to credit bureaus. If you have accounts in good standing with these companies, you should contact them in the hopes of having this information submitted to the credit bureaus and reflected on your account.

If you cannot get the information added to your credit report there is another alternative. Contact the creditor in question and ask the credit manager for a reference letter. This letter should highlight the positive information about your account. Explain that the status of this account does not appear on your credit report and that you would like a document that reflects your ability to borrow and repay.

After you have gone to three or four creditors, you can compile a portfolio of your good credit accounts and show it to any potential creditors when you interview with them or review your application. If they don't schedule an interview, then you should take the initiative and do it yourself. You want the creditor to see these letters before they make a decision about whether to lend you money or not.

The 5 Ways to Get a Bank Loan

"If you give the bank what it needs, the bank will give you all the money you want."

In other words, if the bank needs collateral, a good credit history and a stable employment record, then work on these things until you can show the bank that you have them. It doesn't take long to straighten out most problems and get the money you need.

If you don't have everything that the bank needs to process your loan, then you might want to take advantage of some banking loopholes that can help persuade the bank to give you a loan. Most banks won't tell you about these techniques unless they consider you to be a good credit risk and they want to make the loan.

1. **The bank will lend you five times as much as you have on deposit.** If you have $400 on deposit they will lend you five times that amount ($2,000). They still want you to meet their standards of good credit, good income, and a decent amount of time on the job. You will also need to pledge your $400 savings account as collateral.

2. **A bank will give you a "BIG" loan if you have shown that you can pay off smaller loans from the same bank.** For example, if you borrow $1,000 and then pay it off, you can then go back to the bank and borrow $2,000 and then

$5,000. If you start small, each new loan can almost double in size. If the bank sees that you can pay off small loans, then they will more than likely look at you as a good credit risk. That means that they will extend you more credit each time.

You should work this plan with one bank, but make sure the bank is big enough to continue increasing your credit limit. Once you build up a good reputation for repaying your debts, you can continue this process with other banks. Before long you will have a credit line of over $100,000 or more. Plus, this is also a great way to help build AAA-1 credit.

3. **Get a cosigner who has a strong asset statement and a good credit rating to help you out.** In return, give the person a percentage of the business or 3 to 5 percentage points on the loan. On a $100,000 loan, you would give the cosigner $3,000 to $5,000 for his signature on your loan.

Since he is responsible if you default, he will probably check you out to make sure that you can make the payments on the loan.

4. **The bank will more than likely give you a loan if you are willing to cross collateralize the loan with another form of collateral.** For example, if you want to buy a new car, and you have a used car, you can offer them the new car and your used car as collateral. This gives the bank

officer a sense of security. Plus, this helps to increase your chances of getting the loan.

5. Borrow some else's financial statement to help you out. Have someone else put up some of their assets in order to help you get a loan. For example, let's say that you need a loan to start a business and you don't have a big financial statement or any collateral to show the lender. Find a person who will put up his financial statement and possibly some of his collateral to guarantee the loan.

Unlike a cosigner, this person is usually very well off financially and has a strong financial statement to back up the loan. The only draw back is that this person will take from 40% to 50% or more of the profits.

If you only have a dream and no money, it's a good idea to have a person who is well off help you out. Remember, once you have done one deal you can always go back and do another. It's better to own 40% of something that's bringing you lots of cash, than 100% of nothing.

How to Get Money Even If You Have Bad Credit and No Collateral

I learned about this secret a while back when I needed some money to catch up on some old bills. I went to the bank, filled out a loan application and thought that everything was OK. To my surprise, I was turned down for the loan. The bank wanted something more.

At the time I didn't have perfect credit or any collateral and I was really in need of the loan. They told me that if I could get a cosigner I would get the loan. So, I got a cosigner - my mother. They gave me the loan.

Mom's credit wasn't perfect either, but together it was enough for me to get the loan. Now, I can go back to that bank at anytime and get a loan without a cosigner.

Find a friend or family member who is willing to cosign with you on the loan. You may even want to offer the cosigner a certain amount of money in exchange for their services. Just be sure that you stay current on the loan, otherwise the cosigner will have to pay off the balance of the loan. This is an excellent way to start establishing a good credit rating.

How Banks Rank You

Banks and other lenders look forward to lending money to people who fit their lending requirements. You can make the lender's job a lot easier when you give them what they want to see. You can also make your job infinitely easier when you know beforehand the answers that they are looking for.

Don't think that by knowing the ins and outs of banking, that you will somehow be deceiving the lender. On the contrary, by knowing the inside secrets of banking, you will be doing yourself and the lender a favor. You will get the money you want, and you will give the lender an opportunity to do some additional business.

Banks and credit card companies have a certain standard for rating an individual's credibility when making a loan. Knowing how they rate or score you when you apply will increase your chances of getting the money you want.

So, before you apply for your next loan or credit card, study the chart below and rate yourself. Find out where

you stand and make any adjustments you need to make before you hand in your next application

POINTS SYSTEM

AGE	points	CREDIT HISTORY	points
18 to 21	0	Previous loan at this bank	5
22 to 25	1	Previous loan at another bank	4
26 to 6	2		3
66 to 70	1	Savings account at this bank	2
70+	0	Checking account at this bank	1
		Checking account at	1

		another bank No previous loan experience	
MARITAL STATUS	**points**	**OCCUPATION**	**points**
Married	2	Professional,	5
Single	1	executive	4*
Separated	1	Supervisor,	3*
Widowed	1	government	2
Divorced	1	Skilled	1
		government employee Unskilled Part-time, home worker **Depends on government branch*	
DEPENDENTS*	**points**	**TOTAL MONTHLY INCOME***	**points**
One to four	2	Over $3,001	5
Five to six	1	$2,251 to $3,000	4
Over six	0	$1,501 to $2,250	3
*Include Yourself		$901 to $1,500	2
		Under $900 **Depends on area*	1
LIVING ARRANGEMENTS Own-no mortgage	**points** 5	**PRESENT EMPLOYEMENT** Over 10 years	**points** 5 4

	points		points
Own-mortgage	4	7 to 10 years	3
Rent-unfurnished	2	4 to 7 years	2
Rent-furnished	1	2 to 4 years	1
With parents	1	Under 2 years	

YEARS AT ADDRESS	**points**	**MONTHLY RENT/MORTGAGE**	**points**
Over 6 years	4	Over $750	1
4 to 6 years	3	$500 to $749	2
2 to 3 years	2	Under $500	2
Under 2 years	1		

PREVIOUS ADDRESS	**points**	**MONTHLY EXPENSES***	**points**
Over 6 years		Under $300	3
3 to 5 years	3	$301 to $600	2
Less than 3 years	2	Over $601	1
	1	* Excluding rent or mortgage	

The above chart works for both non-collateral signature loans and credit card applications. If your spouse is employed and signs the application, make sure to include his/her earning in your total monthly income.

A score of 18 points or higher will qualify you for at least a $1,000 loan payable in 24 monthly installments at most banks. The bank will also take into consideration your ability to repay the loan based on your total monthly income from all sources. They will also consider your present outstanding monthly payment obligations.

If you score less than 17 points, there is a good chance that the bank will disqualify you without considering any other factors, even if your income is over $2,000 per month.

More Loan Tips

The first question that usually appears on a loan application asks, "The purpose of the loan." To get quick approval, note what kind of loans the bank happens to be pushing at the time you apply.

Banks and finance companies have "specials" at different times of the year. In July and August they might be pushing vacation loans, in March and April it may be tax loans, and in May and June it might be home repair or auto loans. They have specials all year long. List the loan they are pushing and you'll increase your chances of getting the loan.

Loans that usually get quick approval at any time of year are: auto, home repair, vacation or travel loans, furniture and major appliance loans. You can use almost any reason; as long as the bank thinks that it's for personal use, you will get the loan.

Don't give the bank any reason to give you the run-around. For example, when they ask why you want the loan, don't say to a buy a house, because they will send you to mortgage department. If you put, "to buy a new car," they will want to know who the dealer is. Just put down to buy a privately owned car. This will leave the bank out of your personal affairs. Remember, you don't want to get too personal with the bank until you have started doing some business with them.

How to Get AAA-1 Credit

The best credit reference you can get is one from a bank. If you have $1,000 available, here is a strategy that will quickly help you establish a good credit rating.

1. Take your initial $1,000 and open a savings account at the bank of your choice. After the account has been posted or cleared (which usually takes three days), go back to the bank and ask for a $1,000 loan. Don't worry if you have bad credit. Your collateral will be your savings account. These are called savings secured loans. Be sure to ask the loan officer about any fees associated with this type of loan.

2. Take the $1,000 loan and go to another bank (not just a different branch). Open another savings account. After the account has been posted, take out another $1,000 loan from this bank. Then, go to another bank (not just a different branch) and repeat this process one more time.

3. Now, take the $1,000 loan money and go to a fourth bank. At this bank open a checking account with your $1,000. Next, pay one of the monthly payments on each bank loan. Wait a full week and send in the second wave of monthly

payments. Repeat this process with your third monthly payments.

After you pay off all the loans, get a copy of your credit report and make sure that your latest activities were recorded. When a creditor opens your file, they will see the following:

1. An active checking account.

2. Three $1,000 savings accounts

3. Three $1,000 bank loans that you have paid off ahead of schedule.

This is an excellent way to pave the road to an AAA-1 credit rating. Remember, like everything else we've discussed, do your homework. Don't just walk into any bank and try to secure a loan. Ask questions about interest rates and other fees. This method is valid but you are in charge of its execution. It is up to you to make it work.

Secured Credit Cards: *How to Get One*

In most states, banks are only allowed to charge you 1½ percent on paid balances of your credit card accounts. This comes out to around 18% a year, which is a high interest rate. However, some states consider cash advances on your credit cards as loans. Because these states consider these types of advances to be loans, the bank can only charge 1% interest per month. That's only 12% per year.

How can you use this information to your advantage? Make purchases with your credit card advances, and pay them off about 30 days after you make them. This allows you to make purchases on credit and only pay 1½ percent interest each month. If this law applies to your state, you will be able to cut your credit card expenses by one-third using this method. Please note that some banks apply a service charge to cash advances, in which case, the amount of money you save will be smaller. It is advisable to check with your bank or Credit Card Company before attempting this plan.

If you are having difficulty getting regular credit cards because of your past credit problems, or because of a lack of credit, there is a method that could help you to obtain a credit card. You can obtain a "secured" VISA or MASTERCARD or maybe both.

Open a savings account at one of the many smaller banks that are FSLIC and offer secured credit cards. A secured credit card requires that you deposit a specified amount of money for your Visa or MasterCard. These cards are referred to as secured because the money you deposit is considered security for the amounts you charge with the card.

The money you deposit must remain in the savings account for as long as you retain the card. If you withdraw all your money from the savings account, you must also return the card.

Although this method of obtaining credit may sound extreme, you must remember what your goal is – to obtain unsecured credit. Most places will give you a credit limit equal to the amount you have on deposit. This allows you to literally set your own limit.

Since any loan against your credit card is secured by your savings account, you are in essence, borrowing your own money.

The interest rate on a secured card is generally less (about 10% to 15%) as compared to the 18% to 21% that unsecured credit cards charge.

If you don't live near a small bank, you can write to the nearest one and have them send you all the information you need. Below is a sample letter after which you can draft your own.

SAMPLE Secured Card Letter

June 15, 2007

Lending Institution
123 First Street
Any Town, USA 21100

Dear Sir/Madame:

I am interested in opening a savings account with you in order to obtain a secured VISA or MasterCard. Please send me a credit card application form and other pertinent information regarding your secured credit card program.

Thank you for your time and prompt response.

Sincerely,

Joe Q. Customer

Frequently Asked Questions

Q: My credit report shows transactions from other people with the same or similar name as mine. How can I get it cleaned up?

A: Newspaper stories over the last 25 years have repeatedly highlighted the problem of inaccurate information contained in credit reports. According to some studies, more than 3 in 5 consumers have negative information in their credit report and almost half of those reports contain errors. Some of the errors were serious enough to prevent the individual from qualifying for credit.

If you find yourself in this situation, simply contact the offending credit bureau and submit any relevant information that can prove that the information on your report is inaccurate. Such items include a copy of your driver's license, social security card, and any other information the credit bureau might find useful.

Q: My creditor, to whom I've had late payments, offered to work out a compromised payment plan with a notarized agreement that upon payment, the late payments on my credit report would be deleted? Does this work?

A: This is a common scam offered by credit card companies that is NOT guaranteed to work. There have been numerous people burned by this, because legally companies are

NOT required to remove accurate information (you were late, after all), even if they have made "arrangements".

They may not send you the notarized letter as promised. However, if the company is willing to send the letter first, this might not be a bad idea. Ensure that the letter that they send you states that they made the mistake and that your account was never late.

Q: Are "Credit Repair" agencies legitimate?

A: Most credit repair agencies operate within the law, but don't do anything for you that you cannot do for yourself. Most charge around $800, when you can do the same thing for under $50.00. If you decide to use an agency, be sure you have in writing exactly what they intend to do, including any guarantees they may make. You should think seriously about saving the money and doing the work yourself.

Most credit repair agencies request a copy of your credit report and then challenge any unfavorable items on it, whether they are true or not. The agency does not have to give any reasons. Just a simple, "I challenge this" starts the process. Then the credit bureau begins the process of verifying the information that was challenged.

The ability of credit repair agencies to remove negative information depends on most credit grantors not having the records or simply failing to respond within the credit bureau's time limit. And just like that...Presto! The item is removed. However, if the grantor confirms the item, it stays on your record.

Q: My spouse and I have a joint credit account and he ran up a lot of debt. We've since divorced and I want my ex's debts off my credit.

A: Unfortunately, if the account has both names on it, both parties are responsible for paying the debt. Unless the report is actually in error, there is not much that you can do.

However, you may be able to persuade lenders to give you credit. To do so, you much be able to show that your record was clean prior to marriage, it was your spouse who ran up the debt, and you have arranged with the creditors to pay off the debts over time. It is probably a good idea to visit the credit manager in person to explain your situation. If all else fails, you may still be able to get a secured credit card.

Q: I got in trouble and ran up a lot of debts I couldn't pay. Now my credit report looks terrible. How can I get credit?

A: Most lenders grant credit based on how likely they think you are to pay off the new debt. If you have existing debts that are delinquent, then you're probably not a good risk. The best way to become a good risk is to clear up your credit report.

If your circumstances have changed abruptly (i.e. you've lost your job, experienced major health problems, etc.) it's best to visit your creditors before your accounts become past due. Explain the situation directly; let them know that you intend to pay your debts but need to work out a reduced payment plan. Then make your payments on time. You may also want to consider placing a 100 word statement in your credit file, to explain a period of delinquency caused by some unexpected hardship, a catastrophe, serious illness, or unemployment, which cut off or drastically reduced your income.

Q: The credit bureau ignored my correction – or they say the item is correct and I can prove that it's wrong. What can I do?

A: There are four things you can do. First, you have the right to send the credit bureau a 100 word statement that disputes the item. The bureau is required by law to include that statement in your credit file. When you apply for credit, the lender will see the statement and may take it into consideration.

Second, you can complain to the Federal Trade Commission (FTC). The FTC is the U.S. governmental agency that oversees enforcement of the Fair Credit Reporting Act. If the credit bureau is clearly behaving unreasonably, you can file a complaint with the FTC and they will write to the credit bureau requesting an explanation. In most cases this will prompt the credit bureau to take action.

Third, you can complain to your state government. The consumer protection division of the attorney general's office is a good place to start. Experian settled lawsuits by 14 state attorney generals with a consent decree filed on December 10, 1991. Thus, state governments may be especially interested in hearing if Experian breaks the rules. Equifax and Trans Union are the next logical targets for state governments and the FTC.

Fourth, you can sue for libel or defamation of character. Of course, this is a last resort and will involve paying attorney's fees. However, if you sue a credit agency or user of credit information who willfully or negligently violates the Fair Credit Reporting Act, you can be awarded actual damages, court costs, and attorney's fees, plus punitive damages if the noncompliance was willful.

Q: My credit report shows adverse information, but I have a letter from the bank saying that the information is false. Can I submit this letter to the credit bureau?

A: Yes for Experian and probably not for Trans Union and Equifax.

Industry practice has been that if you dispute an item, the credit bureau ignores any documentation you send in. Instead, the bureau simply asks the credit grantor for verification of the item. Due to increasing pressure from consumer rights advocates however, most credit bureaus are now beginning to use the information you submit to help verify the validity of your claim.

Q: What exactly will the credit bureau do with my correction?

A: In most cases they will send a letter to the credit grantor that originally reported the item to see if it's correct. If the credit grantor says the information is wrong, the item is deleted from your report. If the credit grantor does not respond, the credit bureau should delete the item. If the credit grantor says the information is correct, the credit bureau will let you know.

There are currently no Federal laws setting deadlines for the credit bureau to respond to you. However, in the consent decree filed on December 10, 1991, Experian promised to "verify, delete, or modify any disputed information in a credit report within 30 days after receipt of a complaint."

Currently, there is no way to be sure that a wrong item, once deleted, won't reappear later. However, in the consent decree, Experian promised to change its computer software so that erroneous items won't reappear in subsequent reports.

Q: Is "Credit File Segregation" legitimate?

A: You may have seen the ads that claim you can get a 'New Credit File.' Many of these are scams. These companies have you apply for an Employer Identification Number (EIN), which is almost indistinguishable from a Social Security Number (SSN). You then use this number to establish a new credit account. As long as you never default on your bills, you may just get away with it. However, there are some things you should be aware of:

1. If you have declared bankruptcy and apply for a loan or life insurance for an amount greater than $50K, you must disclose this on the application. If you lie and are caught, your loan could be called or your insurance cancelled.

2. If you default and they find out that you had bad credit under another SSN, you may be prosecuted for felony fraud. Although this method of credit repair my be technically legal, it is so close to fraud that a single mishap on your part might land you in jail.

Q: How long does negative information stay on my credit report?

A: The following is a list of the most common negative items on credit reports and how long each item stays on your report.

- **Delinquencies:** (late payments) made from 30-180 days after their due dates are considered delinquent. They remain on your credit report for 7 years from the date of the missed payment even if you bring your account current later.

- **Collection accounts:** these stay on your credit report for 7 years from the date of the initial missed payment that led to the collection. It is important to remember that even if you pay the account off later it will still stay on your report as "paid collection".

- **Charge-offs:** these items remain on your credit report for 7 years from the date of the initial missed payment that led to the account being charged-off.

- **Closed accounts:** when an account is closed is stays on your credit report for 7 years from the date it was reported closed.

- **Inquiries:** these stay on your credit report for a minimum of 1 year and a maximum of 2 years.

- **Bankruptcies:** chapters 7, 11, and 12 remain on your account for 10 years from the filing date. Chapter 13 bankruptcy stays on file for 7 years from the filing date.

- **Judgments:** child support judgments, civil and small claims judgments remain on your report for 7 years. City, county, state and federal tax liens also remain on your report for 7 years.

All negative information on our credit report will be deleted with time. That gives you the opportunity to resolve your credit problems and rebuild a good credit history. Positive credit information remains on your credit report indefinitely, making your credit report a great benefit for you in obtaining and using financial services.

ONE LAST THING

Real estate is speculative and no one can predict success with 100% accuracy. I, myself do not assume any responsibility for any decisions you make when buying real estate or repairing your credit. Results may vary due to the unique circumstances of each individual. I cannot be responsible for the following;

Earthquakes
Tornados
Fire
Floods
Wind
Heat
Rain
Lost mail
Crazy creditors
Bad Bankers
Falling meteors
Sudden job loss
Crazy tenants
Your stupid mistakes
Or any thing else that might seem like my fault.

This book contains useful information regarding real estate and credit repair. However, it is by no means exhaustive. I encourage the reader to do their own homework. Make sure you learn as much as you can about these topics. Read books, take classes, and ask a lot of questions. Don't purchase more property than you can afford.   Keep at least 3 to 6 months rent in reserve for emergencies.

Fact: 97% of all millionaires achieved their wealth through real estate.

However, these people have had their share of life's problems and setbacks too. Life happens and things don't work out. Nevertheless, they press on in spite of the problems.

Write out your goals. Review them often. Plan your work then work your plan. Prepare to hang in there for the long haul. This may not be a get rich quick path. However, if you stay on the path and overcome the obstacles, the path will lead to success.

God Bless, Be Well, and Find Your WHY!

Rodney & Mark

Don't Miss This SPECIAL OFFER!!!

Everything you have read in this book, we can do for you. Take a look at the programs below.

EquityTRAX - Imagine a system that will show you how to pay off all of your debt, including your mortgage(s) in 1/2 to 1/3 of the time, or even less, without spending any more per month on your debt than you do right now! This CAN be done without qualifying for any new loans or slaughtering your credit rating! That's right! This is NOT a consolidation program or credit counseling program – plain and simple, EquityTRAX is a step-by-step system that will show you your Creditor's Debt Plan, the one making them rich, and your NEW EquityTRAX Plan, the one that will make you WEALTHY!

Here's the bottom line: Your Creditor's Plan was designed to make them rich while they leverage the POWER of your money. Your EquityTRAX Plan turns the tables and puts the POWER back where it belongs. Since both plans cost the exact same amount per month, which plan do you think is better for you and your family?

CreditTRAX - These services are designed to help you improve your past credit history and credit scores back to the best shape possible, settle bad unsecured debts, and give you a fresh start towards improving your overall financial future.

Credit Restoration: This service is designed to correct or delete derogatory information contained on your credit reports with the 3 major credit reporting agencies (Trans Union, Experian, and CSC a.k.a. Equifax). If you have information contained on your credit reports such as: Late Payments, Collections, Judgments, Tax Liens, Repossessions, Charge Offs, Foreclosures, or Bankruptcy Items that you believe may be inaccurate, misleading, outdated, obsolete or no longer able to be verified, **Credit TRAX**, with your authorization, can request that the creditors and credit reporting agencies investigate the validity, accuracy and/or ownership of these accounts. If the accounts you have authorized us to dispute on your behalf are found to be inaccurate or unverifiable, they are required by law to be corrected or deleted from your credit history. Each item deleted or corrected can potentially raise your credit scores, potentially saving you hundreds and even thousands of dollars in interest, down payments and insurance premiums.

Debt Settlement: This service can help you settle BAD Unsecured Debts (Credit Cards, Personal Loans, Medical Collections) for an average of 25-65% of what you owe and allow you to pay your settlements over a 12, 24 or up to 36 month period of time, providing you with the ability to make affordable monthly payments that can fit into your budget and get rid of your Bad Unsecured Debts. This service can also eliminate harassing creditor phone calls, help you to avoid Bankruptcy and potentially save you thousands of dollars in attorney fees, penalties, interest, late fees and even principle. In order to qualify for the **Credit TRAX** Debt Settlement program, you must have at least $8,000 in unsecured debt.

Quick Note: This program does not settle debts that are in good standing, debts on loans or lines of credit that are backed by collateral such as: real estate, automobiles or other forms of personal property or debts that you have already been sued over or have a judgment against you for. This is the best, most affordable and proactive way to resolve your past debt problems, to avoid additional penalties or potential legal action.

Credit Rebuilding: This program can assist you in establishing or reestablishing your credit history. If you have no credit, this program can help you establish a revolving account that will help you develop a credit score. If you have little or no good credit and you would like to reestablish a good pay history to enhance your credit scores, this service can help you accomplish that as well. Based on testimonies provided by existing FDI members that have used this service, they have experienced credit score increases ranging from 5-40 points in as little as 60 days.

Identity Theft Correction Services: By
being an FDI member you have the security
of knowing that you have a professional
credit correction and consulting company in
your corner to help you resolve any problems
that may arise in the event you ever become
a victim of Americas Fastest Growing Crime,
(Identity Theft). Millions of American
consumers have already fallen victim to this
crime and the numbers continue to grow.
USA Today recently had an article that said
the average consumer who becomes a victim
of identity theft spends as much as $1500
and up to 175 hours trying to resolve the
problems that are caused by identity theft.

With *Credit* **TRAX's** Identity theft correction
program, we will help you alleviate any debts
that are set up in your name fraudulently, so
that you are not held responsible for the
repayment of those debts and we will also
make sure that any information that is
reported to your credit file as a result of
identity theft is deleted so that it does not
effect your credit score or your debt to
income ratio. You may have heard of
companies that offer identity theft protection
programs and charge anywhere from $9.95
to $49.95 per month to protect you from
identity theft. If you are an FDI Preferred or
First Class Member you do not need these
services, because our Identity Theft
Correction program is included with your FDI
membership as an absolutely FREE Benefit,
just like all of the other services listed above,
excluding the *Credit* **TRAX** Debt Settlement
Program.

If you are interested in any of these services visit:

www.fdirep.com/monopoly

Or call 866-838-8289

RECOMMENDED WEBSITES

www.rodneytwatson.com
- Earn $$$ While You Learn Real Estate
- Click a Mouse, Buy a House
- We are Investors Creating Investors

www.fdirep.com/monopoly
This site will show you how to have others do everything you read in this book.

www.averageamericanmillionaire.com/monopoly
How to become an Average American Millionaire

Realestatejournal.com – This is the real estate section of the Wall Street Journal. It has useful information and articles.

Real-estate-online.com – This site has helpful information for investors. You can join discussions and ask questions.

Bankrate.com – Here you can get the all current interest rates.

RECOMMENDED READING

Rich Dad, Poor Dad: What the Rich Teach
Their Kids About Money--That the Poor and
Middle Class Do Not!
by Robert T. Kiyosaki, Sharon L. Lechter

Cashflow Quadrant: Rich Dad's Guide to
Financial Freedom
by Robert T. Kiyosaki, Sharon L. Lechter

The Millionaire Next Door: The Surprising
Secrets of Americas Wealthy
Thomas J. Stanley, William D. Danko

Richest Man in Babylon
by George S. Clason

The Science of Getting Rich
By Wallace D Wattles

As A Man Thinketh
By James Allen

APPENDIX

Sample Letter #1

Request a copy of your credit report. Not in response to a credit denial.

January 1, 2007

Experian Inc.
PO Box 2104
Allen, TX 75103

To Whom It May Concern:

In accordance with the Fair Credit Reporting Act, I am requesting that your Credit Bureau send me a copy of my credit report. I have included the required fee of $8.00. Please send the report to the address below:

Joe C. Customer

1234 Main Street

Any Town, USA 11111

My social security number is 123-45-6789 and my date of birth is April 3, 1970.

(Select one of the following as appropriate.)

I have lived at the above address for more than 5 years.

OR

I have lived at the above address for less than 5 years. My former address was 321 Some Street, Out There, USA 12121.

Also enclosed is a copy of my driver's license as proof of my identity.

Thank you for your time and your prompt reply to this request.

Sincerely,

Joe C. Customer

Note: Be sure to sign your letter as the signature is needed in order to process your request.

Sample Letter #2

Request a copy of your credit report within 30 days of a credit denial.

January 1, 2007

Experian Inc.
PO Box 2104
Allen, TX 75103

To Whom It May Concern:

I was denied credit within the past 6 months by *(insert name of company)* and as I understand, your Credit Bureau was the agency responsible for issuing my credit profile. Therefore, in accordance with the Fair Credit Reporting Act, I am requesting that your Credit Bureau send me a free copy of my credit report. Please send the report to the address below:

Joe C. Customer

1234 Main Street

Any Town, USA 11111

My social security number is 123-45-6789 and my date of birth is April 3, 1970.

(Select one of the following as appropriate.)

I have lived at the above address for more than 5 years.

OR

I have lived at the above address for less than 5 years. My former address was 321 Some Street, Out There, USA 12121.

Also enclosed is a copy of my driver's license as proof of my identity.

Thank you for your time and your prompt reply to this request.

Sincerely,

Joe C. Customer

Sample Letter #3

Challenging information on your credit report.

January 1, 2007

Experian Inc.
PO Box 2104
Allen, TX 75103

Re: File #987-65-432

To Whom It May Concern:

I recently received the copy of my credit report sent on December 27, 2007. In my review of the report, I noticed numerous errors concerning various accounts. I have noted these errors directly on the report and have enclosed all relevant proof of my claim.

Please rectify these errors immediately and send me an updated copy of my credit report.

Thank you for your time and your prompt reply to this request.

Sincerely,

Joe C. Customer

Sample Letter #4

Sample 100 word statement explaining your side of a credit dispute.

January 1, 2007

Experian Inc.
PO Box 2104
Allen, TX 75103

Re: File #987-65-432

To Whom It May Concern:

On November 15, 2006, I wrote to you concerning a negative item on my credit report and requested an updated copy of the report once the problem was resolved.

I recently received the updated copy of my credit report and noticed that ABC Market still claims that I owe them $400.00.   As expressed previously, this debt has been paid in full.

Please challenge this item once more and have it removed from my credit report. If ABC Market still does not agree with me, please include the follow 100 word statement in my credit file in accordance with my rights under the FCRA.

"I have paid in full my debt to ABC Market, but for some unknown reason, their records do not reflect this. Payment was made by a third party check, and perhaps, this is too complicated for their record keeping. In any event, I maintain that this account is closed."

Thank you for your time and your prompt reply to this request.

Sample Letter #5

Request for names and addresses of remaining creditors.

January 1, 2007

Experian Inc.
PO Box 2104
Allen, TX 75103

Re: File #987-65-432

To Whom It May Concern:

I have been in contact with your agency concerning my credit file. There are still several negative items on my credit report that are in error and I would like to discuss these items directly with the creditors involved.

As such, I am requesting that you send me the names and addresses of each of these creditors; I am aware that this is a customer right guaranteed by the FCRA.

Enclosed is a copy of my credit report on which I have highlighted the names of the companies in question.

Thank you for your time and your prompt reply to this request.

Sample Letter #6

Negotiating a settlement with each creditor.

January 1, 2007

Mr. Dan Mann
ABC Market
933 Stone Drive

Hometown, USA 22354

Dear Mr. Mann,

The purpose of this letter is to rectify our long standing dispute over whether or not I have paid to you a $400.00 balance.

My statement of the facts is as follows: In March of last year, I made a purchase of $400.00 in your establishment. Soon after, I paid the bill in full by means of a third party check. The third party, who has since moved away and whom I can no longer contact, owed me $400.00. The check given me was endorsed and sent to your company. At that time, one of your employees accepted the check and it was subsequently cashed.

I maintain that I owe you nothing. However, in order to remove this black mark from my credit report, I am willing to work out the following compromise with you.

I will pay you $100.00 up front and make two monthly payments of $50.00 each for a total of $200.00 (half of the disputed amount). In return, I ask that you have this item removed from my credit report as soon as you are in receipt of the initial $100.00 payment. To do so, will require that you write Experian Information Services explaining that you are withdrawing the claim and would like the item deleted from my report.

If you agree with this proposal, please sign this agreement and return it to me.

Sincerely,

Joe C. Customer

Agreed to by:_____ on _____

Sample Letter #7

Request for distribution of your updated credit report.

January 1, 2007

Experian Inc.
PO Box 2104
Allen, TX 75103

Re: File #987-65-432

To Whom It May Concern:

On November 30, 2006, I believe that ABC Market contacted you stating that they were dropping their claim against me and wanted the item removed from my credit report. I respectfully request that you do so.

When corrected, please be so kind as to send me a copy of my updated credit report in addition to those companies that requested my credit report in the past 6 months.

Thank you for your time and your prompt reply to this request.

Sincerely,

Joe C. Customer

(SAMPLE) Option to Purchase Real Estate

THIS AGREEMENT made by and between

_____

(hereinafter called "Optionor") and

_____,

(hereinafter called "Optionee").

OPTIONED PROPERTY: Optionor, in consideration of the payment of an option fee under this Option Agreement, hereby grants to Optionee the right and option to purchase the premises below at any time during the term of this agreement, and subject to the covenants and conditions hereinafter set forth, the following described property: _____

_____.

Together with all improvements thereon, all privileges, appurtenances, easements and all fixtures, presently situated in said building except the following:

_____

_____

_____.

1. **TERM:** The term of this Agreement shall be _____ months beginning on the first day of _____ and ending on the last day of _____, 20___.
2. **OPTION FEE:** Optionee agrees to pay $_____ as a NON-REFUNDABLE FEE, as consideration for the Optionor to grant the Option to Optionee to purchase the above premises.
3. **OPTION PRICE:** The option price of the Property shall be $_____

The Option Fee as provided in Paragraph 2 above shall be refunded to the Optionee to be used only as a down payment upon the purchase of the Property, as said Option Fee is NON-REFUNDABLE in the event that Optionee does not exercise the Option and purchase the Property.

4. **Assignment of Option**. Optionor agrees that Optionee may assign this agreement to a third-party. Optionor will allow the Optionee to show the property to potential assignees by giving appropriate notice to the Optionor.

5. **TERMS OF THE OPTION:** Optionee may at any time during this term enter into an agreement of sale with the Optionor to purchase the property at the price specified in Paragraph 2. Optionee will arrange their own financing and pay all closing costs connected with the transfer of the property and obtaining the loan, so that the sale or exchange can be completed in sixty (60) days of the exercise of the option. Optionor agrees to deliver a good and sufficient General Warranty Deed conveying a marketable title to said property to the Optionee.

6. **BINDING EFFECT:** This Option and the agreements contained herein shall be binding upon inure to the benefit of heirs, executors, administrators, successors and assigns of the respective parties.

7. **DISCLOSURES:** Optionee acknowledges receipt of the "Residential Property Disclosure" statement, the EPA "Disclosure of Information on Lead-Based Paint and Lead-Based Paint Hazards" statement, and the EPA "Protect Your Family From Lead In Your Home" booklet. and understands their contents.

8. **MISCELLANEOUS:** Optionee agrees that they have examined the title to the Property and found no errors in the title and hereby accepts all assessments and encumbrances upon the property.
9. **APPLICABLE LAW:** This agreement shall be interpreted according to the Laws of the State of California.

IN WITNESS WHEREOF, Optionor and Optionee have executed this agreement on the _____ day of _____, 20_____.

OPTIONER _____

OPTIONER_____

OPTIONEE_____

OPTIONEE_____

Witness: _____ Date: _____

Good Luck!